T
 H
  O
   U
    G
     H
      T
       S

for the

Listening

H E A R T

A Collection of Prayers as Poems by
Thomas J. Rillo

Thomas J. Rillo

Cover: Triptych painted by Br. Martin Erspamer, OSB, of Saint Meinrad Archabbey. Photo by the author.

Thoughts for the Listening Heart

DEDICATION

Dedicated to the Benedictine Oblates of Saint Meinrad Archabbey who have proclaimed and practiced the Christian virtues of faith, hope, and charity and seek to grow closer to God.

ACKNOWLEDGMENTS

In writing this collection of poems I have had the support and guidance of many who have supported me in the endeavor. First and foremost was the Holy Spirit who placed the words in my mind and guided me to put them into poetic format. Without the Spirit's help there would be no book.

Second to the Holy Spirit is my wife Joan who has supported me and advised me as both editor and computer support. She put in countless hours editing, typing and organizing the poems into a book format. Without her love, her unselfish efforts, this endeavor would never have met fruition.

Special thanks to Mark Hooker and Stella Hooker-Haase for their generous encouragement and support with the necessary organizational and computer publishing skills. Thanks also to *The Criterion*, newspaper of the Archdiocese of Indianapolis, for publishing over these past few years some of the poems appearing in this book.

My gratitude goes to Saint Meinrad Archabbey in Indiana and to St. Charles Borromeo Church in Bloomington, Indiana, for infusing within me the heightened spirituality reflected in these poems. Also, a very sincere appreciation is extended to many of my fellow parishioners at St. Charles for their continual encouragement with regard to my poetry.

May God always shed His grace upon all of you.

——Bloomington, Indiana, Winter 2011

TABLE of CONTENTS

LIVING ICONS OF CHRIST

A Holy Man from Zimbabwe

He was a devout and holy man from Zimbabwe
An African priest with an angelic countenance
His transatlantic journey fueled by a musical quest
Seeking a university degree in madrigal studies.

Obligation to celebrate Mass placed him in our Church
His celebration of Mass was a cultural experience
His voice resonating with a beautiful tonal quality
An aura of holiness radiated from a postural stance.

Joy was a constant expression in a serene smile
He wore a cloak of humility as a badge of honor
Often he accompanied the cantor in song
Providing syncopated beats on handcrafted drums.

Drums he handcrafted in the tradition of his homeland
Charismatic sound echoing throughout the Church
Like the psalms of praising God with lyre and harp
He exemplified praise of God with rhythmic drumbeats.

Years spent with us were more precious than gold
By example he taught about embracing diversity
Recalled by his bishop for priestly duties at home
We all miss him beyond conceivable measurement.
His name was Emanuel--meaning God with us.

(This poem was written with respect and admiration for a wonderful priest.)

A Man of Hate to One of Love

The old Saul the Holy Spirit desired to transform
Violent, blaspheming, zealous and persecuting
Witness to Stephen's persecution and death
Meeting Jesus on the road to Damascus
He was struck to the ground by a blinding light
A man of hate to one of love

The persecutor rose and experienced blindness
From blindness to sight the transformation began
The Holy Spirit moving him from hate to love
His transformation was the greatest of gifts to all
A man of hate to one of love

He was aided by Paul's struggles with a fallen nature
Pharisee to preacher he became apostle to the Gentiles
Moved from a self-centered to Christ-centered approach
A man of hate to one of love

Drank in the wine of God and then gave it to others
He kept the faith in the face of intimidating odds
He brought the Gospel to the Jews and the Gentiles
He never lost his courage in fighting the good fight
A man of hate to one of love

(This poem was inspired in commemo-
ration of Pope Benedict's declaration that
2008-2009 be the year of St. Paul.)

A Priest Forever

His was a life of long commitment to the search for God
Ordained as a shepherd to the faithful of his flock
His ministry extended to the unfaithful as well
He saw Christ in all he encountered.
A priest forever

The values he held so close were basic and proven
Honesty and truth were prioritized in his mind
He was an original from a past generation
Familial ties ever so strong in his life.
A priest forever

Beneath a veneer of toughness and worldliness
Was found a heart so ever generous and kind
The heartwood of his soul so visible to those
Who really took time to know him
A priest forever

He touched many lives in his long career
Helping all those who came to him in need
An open door policy reflected in his face
He was a consummate shepherd to the core
A priest forever

Goodbye to our pastor and good friend
You ran the good race despite the hurdles
Of debilitating afflictions of illness and age
A priest forever

Apostle to the Gentiles

Admired for his missionary work and personal transformation

His transformation was a great gift surpassing other gifts

From the time of his dramatic conversion he kept the faith

He left the man of hate behind and
became a man of love.

Apostle to the Gentiles

Beaten, stoned, jailed and maligned he
    became all the stronger
He taught people how to love each other
    by the love of Christ
He teamed up with Barnabas to build up
    the Church of God
Showing others how to grow in holiness
    as a Church family.
Apostle to the Gentiles

Paul was one of a kind set apart for God in every way

From his calling he brought the Gospel to both Jews and Gentiles

With his followers he became a master builder of the Church

He kept the faith and he won the race never wavering from faith.

Apostle to the Gentiles

He drank of the wine of God and then gave it away to others

Established early small churches and Eucharistic celebrations

Preached and evangelized to the far corners of the known world

Martyrdom was both his fate and a gift from God on high.

Apostle to the Gentiles

(Pope Benedict's declaration of the Pauline year led to this poem.)

Icons of the Living Christ

Somewhere between childhood and adulthood
A young man decides to become a priest
Ordination and initial service as an icon of Christ
Seeing both the privilege and burden of the calling.
Icons of the Living Christ

Called to mediate the presence of Christ in the world
To be an icon of Christ in celebration of the Mass
The altar of their ministry is the Eucharist
Offering the bread of life and the cup of salvation.
Icons of the Living Christ

Priests feed the soul and give it strength for the journey
They assist in preparing our souls to appear before God
They show us how to take hold of the salvation
Salvation that Jesus won for us by dying on the cross.
Icons of the Living Christ

Priests called to double ministry of word and sacrament
They serve as reconciler, healer, teacher and friend
Priests help us to understand that each one of us
Has been consecrated as an icon of Christ in the world.
Icons of the Living Christ

(This poem was inspired by the declaration of Year of the Priest.)

In the Footsteps of Saint Paul

Paul, the ardent persecutor of early Christians
Always ready to pursue, punish and confine
Till one day on the way to seek more to punish
He was struck from his mount by a light divine.

Blinded he fell to the ground and heard Jesus
Saul! Saul! Why do you persecute me?
Cured of blindness by a believer, he in turn
Became afire with new faith and began to see.

Eager to preach the Word he began his outward
    reach
Missionary journeys that took him to far places
Seeking the displaced Christians he once hunted
Endured many hardships and threatening menaces.

Mission tenure at Antioch accompanied by Barnabas
Travels to Derbe and Lystra to enlist Timothy
Received a vision of a Macedonian who begged him
Come over to Macedonia and teach us fervently.

Spoke against pagan adherence to an unknown God
Trial by Roman governor in Athens adverted
Continuing evangelizing at Corinth, Ephesus, Philippi
Baptizing Lydia, the first European converted.

Only Jesus Can Make a Priest

Priests are God's own human sacraments,

      Responding to the call of priesthood.

They provide a window to see the Lord,

      The depth and beauty of God's grace flows through it.

To become a priest is not accomplished alone,

      Ordination in itself is a sacrament.

The priest becomes an instrument of Jesus,

      Bringing the Lord's forgiveness in reconciliation.

The priest presents bread and wine to God for change,

      Into the Lord's own body and blood.

Called to anoint the sick and bring the Lord's comfort,

      Giving comfort to the suffering and the dying.

Only Jesus can make a priest to be his instrument,

      Because Jesus was tested through suffering.

So too priests have that humanity through testing,

      That allows them to identify with those seeking help.

(This poem was inspired by witnessing the ordination of priests.)

His Name Was Paul

He was a man who persecuted the Christians
      Relentless in his pursuit of delegated mission
He was a representative of the secular institution
      In prestige, notoriety, power but never submission.

On the road to Damascus God initiated His deed
      To a man who subjected others to the law
A bolt of lightning knocked him off his steed
      The conversion message he clearly saw.

Saul was his name and he listened to Jesus' call
      Jesus gave him His trust when others did not
To go and follow Him and preach salvation to all
      His intent was firm and evangelization his lot.

Obeying the command to bring the word to all nations
      He was kicked out of towns and beaten by his kinsman
Undaunted he preached arduously for conversions
      Humiliated for the Gospel and he never ran.

Power of conversion propelled him on a spiritual trace
      Known for his statement near the end of his life
To have fought the fight and finished the race
      He kept the faith through all of tribulations and strife.

(Inspiration for this poem was derived from Pope Benedict's declaration of the Year of St. Paul.)

A Brother is:

A man who has listened to Christ's call to be truly a brother
    that seeks to relate to others like a real brother helping siblings
        who strives to affirm that we are all members of God's order
            he strives to witness Christ's presence in all human beings.

The brother chooses to live out of chastity, obedience and poverty
    a life lived in the context of community and service to the Church
        a lifestyle that challenges the emphasis on material subjectivity
            community is the key be it monastic or secular in his search.

A vocation chosen that is right by listening to God's quiet call
    God speaks gently to the religious brother within the ear of his heart
        prayerful listening and openness to His will helps him to stand tall
            obedience to listening a vow to do God's will and not be apart.

A brother is a foot soldier who works in the embattled trenches
    recognition and credit are not always a complimentary factor
        the limelight is dim and the spotlight radiance not always drenches
            he accepts his lifestyle and seeking God without visible rancor.

(This poem is in remembrance of a late Sacred Heart brother who served in the community.)

The Good Seminarian

Born of pious and devout parents
Early exposure to the rituals of the Mass
Influenced by the power of prayer
Childhood years too soon pass.
The Good Seminarian

Role models consistently surround him
Continually climbing the parochial school ladder
Daily association with Church traditions
Embracing only spiritual values that matter.
The Good Seminarian

Constantly subjected to positive experience
Faith and family shape his journey to God
Faith that began as a rivulet growing in strength
Like a strong current flowing straight as a rod.
The Good Seminarian

The spiritual current carries him onward
Joined by confreres as mutual support for each other
The deaconate comes first followed by ordination
He becomes an icon of Christ and of the Father.
The Good Seminarian

(Inspiration for the poem came from friendship with a young parishioner and seminarian at Saint Meinrad Theological Seminary.)

What is a Nun?

From the innocence of childhood to the advent of maturity
A woman discerns the call of God to become His bride
The answer is seldom simple and often very complex
Spiritual messages from the Holy Spirit never subside.

Seeking advice from family and friends is never enough
Pastors and parochial teachers give their honest counsel
The final decision is seldom easy and often tough
Questions and anxieties mount like a groundswell.

Knowing at last the right course to undertake
She enters a community of kindred devout women
Formation and final vows finally become a reality
A vocation accepted and waiting to be risen.

Assignments of many locations are varied and diverse
Always seeking God whether in teaching or nursing
Work and prayer routinely embraced with enthusiasm
Seeing Christ in all to whom she ministers is never ending.

Joyful celebration of many years of service to others
She returns to the motherhouse for prayer and contemplation
Participation in the prayer life of the community a blessing
Continuing to seek Father, Christ and Holy Spirit through imitation.

(This poem is in recognition of the fine influence of nuns.)

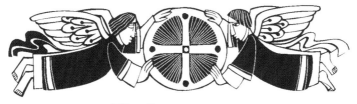

The Last Homily

He steps up to the ambo with oxygen tank in tow
St. Elmo he calls the life-giving device
It gives him aid to inhale and then to blow
He puts forth his words with great sacrifice.

His step falters and his ruddy face goes pale
He looks out at the pews with engaging smile
He begins his personal homiletic tale
His personal obstacles overcome for awhile.

Prayers of the faithful he engaged without formality
Each prayer delivered with individual attention
Each person considered with expressed humility
Each prayer embraced with love and consideration.

We will always remember this priest with fondness
His simplicity of character born of Celtic origin
Aware that this was his last homily, a final address
His final goodbye was silent and contained within.

(This poem was inspired by remembrance of the last weekday Mass celebrated by the writer's late pastor and friend.)

He is a Stone for the Ages

He was a stone of fidelity to his faith
Taken prematurely to heaven's gate.
He was strong and resilient like a stone
Our departed pastor was stone-like in faith.
He is a stone for the ages

His genuine love of children was evident
In appreciation of their spontaneous play.
Appropriate is the place for a memorial
Where children are able to play in freedom.
 He is a stone for the ages

A stone selected for its indigenous origin
Like our late pastor born a native son.
Limestone formed in layers of past life
He too was layered with a passion for life.
He is a stone for the ages

Limestone a source of regional stability
So was his support for those seeking faith.
The stone rejected by the builders transformed
Into a cornerstone for a faith community.
He is a stone for the ages

The stone never viewed as a life form
Life forms gave it the status of formation.
Our former pastor was an icon of Christ
Working always in the vineyard of spirituality.
His was a stone for the ages

(This poem was written for the dedication of the memorial stone
placed in memory of Father Charlie Chesebrough on the St.
Charles School playground.)

14

MINISTERS OF GOD'S WORD

Bernadette of Lourdes

I am the Bread of Life

Sacrament of Inherent Beauty

The Cantor Sang On

The Christian Undertaker

The Forgotten Chalice

The Spirituality of a Lector

What is a Eucharistic Minister

Unheralded Servants of the Lord

The Three Shepherd Children of Fatima

Reflections in an Empty Church

Bernadette of Lourdes

Bernadette must have gasped in wonder
At the task the Virgin Mary entrusted to her
To be heralded
By the mother of God
Who represented God's generosity and love
A task that would reach out to all pilgrims

Did she quail
From accepting such a request from the eternal divinity
To an earthy child's immortality

Did she hesitate
At the sight of the Virgin Mother before her
Fearing that she would not be able to do as she was asked

Then resolutely
The Virgin Mary's voice broke upon Bernadette
Resounding deeply within her child-like heart
In the fertile silence of her soul
So that Mary's request might be planted there
Like a seed in a fertile field

Did she act
Following the Virgin Mary's dictate
To plant a stick in among the rocks
To bring forth the healing waters' flow
To see that a Church be built upon the holy site
So that pilgrims might come from afar to process
In honor of the Virgin Mother
To be healed by the waters of Lourdes.

(This poem was inspired by a pilgrimage to Lourdes in France.)

I am the Bread of Life

Lying quietly on the sanctuary shelf
I am nothing but unleavened bread
Packaged together with my brethren
I am nothing but water, wheat and oil.
I am the bread of life to be

With others of my kind I have been chosen
Chosen by the Grace of God to undergo change
Removed from the package we fall into a bowl
Waiting for a blessing as consecration.
I am the bread of life to be

We are placed upon the holy altar
Representative of Christ initiates the change
Metamorphosis from water, wheat and oil
Transubstantiated through the words of the priest.
I am the bread of life

I become the body of God's son
No longer are am I just a lowly wafer
Elevated my old form is changed
And by God's Grace to feed His people.
I am the bread of life

(All aspects of the Eucharist have always inspired the poet.)

19

Sacrament of Inherent Beauty

The Eucharist is central to our spiritual life
Our faith is awakened by the sound of God's word
We are all nourished at the table of the Eucharist
The celebration of the Eucharist is inherently beautiful.

It is not the food of the Eucharist that is changed into us
But rather we who are mysteriously transformed by it
Christ nourishes us by uniting us with Him
His redeeming sacrifice is present in every Eucharist.

Through the gift of the Eucharist we share in God's inmost life
The Eucharist is the paramount sign of God's presence
His presence is the wellspring of what our souls desire
His Son comes to meet us during the Eucharistic adoration.

The Eucharist is more than just central to our faith
Embracing our everyday existence and making perception possible
Through grace to see the reflection of the Son of God in others
It establishes that the risen Lord is still with us in every moment.

(Awe and love of the Eucharist inspired this poem.)

The Cantor Sang On

When we leave Mass early
  from singing that is divine,
Our appreciation and respect will be fruitless
  like the branch without the vine.

Our parish is blessed with musical talent
  voices of angelic quality resound,

Like incense the notes rise upward
  praises for God through song abound.

It is easy to say we have to leave early
  the procession down the aisle has begun,
To beat the crowd of the faithful departed
  the cantor sings on while we run.

There are churches today that are silent
  no beautiful voices there to sing out,

We are blessed to praise God with music
  it makes our journey of faith more devout.

Let us stand for a few minutes as the cantor finishes
  kneel for awhile in reverent prayer,
The cantor will see our appreciation and respect
  look in your pew and know that God is there.

The Christian Undertaker

He comes to daily Mass in business attire
    A young man with a kind countenance
Love of the Lord burns like a consuming fire
    The greeting of peace is extended in jubilance.

His compassion for the deceased clearly evident
    The funeral mass is blessed by his unceasing care
The survivors are treated with true endearment
    His participation in the Mass is without fanfare.

A hand placed on the casket in subtle manner
    Coordination with the celebrant a top priority
Singing of the processional hymn in a whisper
    All are signs of a Christian undertaker's spirituality.

The church community is blessed by his love
    Grief tempered by a faith strong in his vocation
An earthly duty to the deceased guided from above
    Support to all left behind as strong as a stanchion.

(A parishioner/funeral director handles many parish funeral arrangements.)

The Forgotten Chalice

High in the back of a cabinet shelf
Sits a forgotten chalice in a bed of dust
Tarnished and burnished in color
Forgotten and left in the sacristy.

       The forgotten chalice

Once it went forth from its sanctuary
With regularity and held the wine
To be consecrated in elevation
Praying hands held it high in celebration.

       The forgotten chalice

Whose hands held the chalice on high
How many years had the chalice sat
On the altar as a vital part of the Eucharist
What man of God utilized the vessel.

       The forgotten chalice

Did the chalice cease to serve the faithful
In unison with the servant of the Lord
Did it have subsequent masters who used it
Did just one master pass on with the chalice.

       The forgotten chalice

How many lips touched the rim of the chalice
To take in the strength of the Lord's blood
The chalice sits forgotten awaiting resurrection
To hold again the precious blood of Christ.

       The forgotten chalice

(Inspiration for this poem came upon discovery of a forgotten chalice and reflecting on the memory of the late priest who used it.)

The Spirituality of a Lector

The spirituality of the lector is
    intimacy with the scriptures
    nourished by the word of God
    letting the scriptures enter the heart.

The lector approaches to the scriptures with
    compassion and love
    sensitivity to the need for goodness
    mature understanding of the scriptures.

The lector reads and speaks with
    an intimacy with the risen Christ
    a divine communication in human words
    a message of unconditional love
    focus from the heart to the hearts of others.

The ministry of the lector includes
    the encounter between faith and the risen Lord
    regular exposure to the word of God
    humility in accepting the role of conveying God's word
    knowing that the lector is a minister of the word of God.

What is a Eucharistic Minister

A Eucharistic Minister is
>> an example of Christian living in faith
>> the light of the risen Christ in the light of the Eucharist
>> an instrument of nourishment to those who embrace Christ
>> a representative of the presence of Christ to the people

A Eucharistic Minister has
>> a calling to be the hands of Christ
>> a unique relationship with the Eucharist
>> a tangible sense of quiet joy as a servant
>> a deepening intimacy with the risen Lord

A Eucharistic Minister does
>> evoke the Holy in the midst of the ordinary
>> demonstrate the love of God and neighbor
>> bring the host to those unable to attend Mass
>> nourish the hunger people have for the Eucharist

A Eucharistic Ministry includes
>> knowledge that the Eucharist mystery is beyond understanding
>> realization that the body and blood is the whole person of Christ
>> special awareness of the real presence of Christ
>> reaching out to nourish the faith of all the dispersed faithful

Unheralded Servants of the Lord

Moving quietly and without overt fanfare
Average parishioners never know they are there
Accepting assignments with unconditional love
Knowing they are only noticed by the Lord above.
Sacristans of the Church

Seasonal decorations magically appear
Announcing Advent as it draws near
Accouterments of the Passion of the Lord
Magically materialize with harmony and accord.
Sacristans of the Church

Candles seem to be perpetually giving light
Mysteriously dispelling darkness of night
Each candle serviced by an unheralded servant
Tasks such Church candles are very important.
Sacristans of the Church

Towels and linens give support to the Eucharist
Clean and fresh smelling like the morning mist
All made possible by the humble servants of the Lord
Sacristan is service to the Church and to God's word.
Sacristans of the Church

The Three Shepherd Children of Fatima

Three young children tending their sheep
Enjoying freedom of work and play
Secure in stability and familial love
When an angel of God appeared to them.

The angel taught the children to pray
How to pray the Eucharistic prayer
The Mother of Jesus appeared before them
Her clothing glowed in radiant white light.

The children stood transfixed with wonder
The Virgin Mary spoke to them in strong tones
She spoke to the children words of tranquil hope
Her directions were firm and clearly discernible.

The Lady of the Rosary revealed three secrets
The oldest child was able to understand and interpret
Vision of hell and salvation was described to the child
Death of the Pope and other religious was included.

Gathered villagers viewed the miracle of the sun
Layers of clouds cloaked the silver disc of it
The silver sun was enveloped in gauzy gray light
The sun whirled and turned into the broken clouds.

Six times the Virgin Mother appeared to the oldest
All three were doubted, interrogated without kindness
Believed by the Church and the Virgin Mary's request
Fatima was born as a holy site for all generations.

(Inspiration for this poem occurred at a pilgrimage to Fatima, Portugal.)

Reflections in an Empty Church

The church is completely empty except for me
For there has to be someone to hear the echoes
This is the end of the week and Masses have ended
I sit in the pew and reflect on what has ensued.

The sounds of the prayers linger in space
The prayers of both young and old remain
Inaudible except to the ear of the heart
The smell of incense is perceptible to the nose.

Bits of candy wrappers rest beneath the kneelers
Pacifiers for the inattentiveness of young children
A forgotten rosary lies on the wood of the pew
A child's spiritual comic book rests in the rack.

Voices raised in glory and praise for the Lord
Remain entrenched in the folds of a banner
A daily missal left behind in the exit confusion
Church bulletins read and left behind after mass.

The church slumbers echoing the sounds of worship
The cantor's voice and proclamation of the readings
Are indelibly etched in the fabric of the church's ambience
I sit quietly and reflect for I am the priest and pastor.

(Inspiration came from watching his pastor praying in church late on Sunday afternoon.)

HE HEARS OUR PRAYERS

A Strong and Powerful Joy

By Way of the Desert

My Prayer Closet

Praying in the Desert

The Light Through the Cross

Through the Stained Glass Window

When I Pray in Church

The Narrow Door to Heaven

Gateway to Renewed Life

A Strong and Powerful Joy

A strong and powerful joy
   Seizes me
As my journey to God
    Draws me ever closer to Him
The joy trickles slowly downward
    To my swelling heart
In the silence of prayer
    Humility prevails
My deep acceptance
    A permeating acceptance
Fueled by a love of God
    The sacredness of His love
Mends my brokenness.

(This poem developed during a meditation in the silence of the church.)

By Way of the Desert

They wanted to grow ever closer to God
To escape the depravities and sins of the city
Leaving behind the distractions of ordinary life
Focusing on salvation to seek a purer spirituality.
By Way of the Desert

The Fertile Crescent was never far from desert wilderness
They were a people familiar with dry sand and hot sun
Encounters with God resulted in this silent wilderness
The harsh desert where relationship with God was won.
By Way of the Desert

They were called the desert fathers and mothers
Followers addressed them as abbas and ammas
Designations of high regard and not just lofty titles
They were hermit monks with a strong faith and lofty vistas.
By Way of the Desert

They founded the first monastic communities
St. Anthony's cave became the earliest monastery
Followed by St. Catherine Monastery at Mt. Sinai
The birth of monasticism occurred in the desert nursery.
By Way of the Desert

(A visit to St. Catherine Monastery at Mt. Sinai during a pilgrimage to Egypt
brought this poem to mind.)

My Prayer Closet

A closet is a simple small space
Used for the storage of things not in use
Things that are needed for the rat race
To be extracted from their recluse.

The closet is windowless and devoid of light
Sounds are muffled and silence prevails
The chaotic world is shut off and out of sight
Peace and tranquility is the closet's rail.

So too is my mind like the proverbial closet
It provides storage for things to be used or not
I can control its intake or its outlet
My mind can become a sanctuary prayer spot.

I can be still and listen to God
I can shut the door of my closet mind
Intrusions and distractions are not ramrods
Only my prayers are permitted to bind.

My prayer closet can be located anywhere
On a busy sidewalk or in a public space
The door can be closed and prayers are in there
My mind as a prayer closet joins me in life's race.

In the midst of the urban secular scene
I can retreat to the prayer closet of my mind
There I can listen to God in tones so serene
To pray in silence protected from humankind.

Praying in the Desert

To live in the desert is very arduous so I am told
Desert mystics did so for purification and courage
Jesus went to the desert to pray and fast for forty days
Scripture tells us that it was preordained that way.

The desert is more than a geographical expression
To the pilgrim the desert symbolizes intercession
In the desert the Spirit expresses the search for God
Search for God in silence that animates God's word.

It is a suspension bridge spanning the crevasses of temptation
Enabling the soul in love with God to cross the dark abyss

>   Over the unfathomable precipices of
>   one's own fears
>   That form obstacles to the progress
>   of the journey to God.

>   Such desert is holy and a prayer
>   beyond all prayer
>   It leads to the continuous presence
>   of God
>   Contemplation achieves a greater
>   height for the soul at peace

The desert in my life is more than a geographical place.

We must create the desert in the heart of crowded places
The sidewalk becomes a corridor leading to my desert
Travel in a vehicle can be a place of quiet meditation
If one cannot go to the desert the desert may come to us.

(Inspiration for this poem came from an intensified and chaotic urban
experience and from a study of the desert mystics.)

The Light Through the Cross

It hung high above the altar of God,
It was a large transparent cross with a corpus.
A beam of sunlight coming through a rear window
Forming a circle of light on the floor before the altar.

The light through the cross shines for each of us
Knowledge that Jesus dispelled the darkness.
He illuminated the world with the light of salvation
We move toward the sanctuary into the circle of light.

Light from the east is transported on the light beam
Its magnifying force pulling us to the Eucharistic feast.
Each of us in turn steps humbly into the circle of light
Hands turned upward to receive His body.

His real presence is transported on the beam of light
We are warmed with the light radiating through the cross.
Absorbing the light we evangelize in His name
The light through the cross always sustains us.

(Inspiration for this poem came from attending Mass at Maria Goretti Church,
Scottsdale, AZ.)

Through the Stained Glass Window

The church is quiet and veiled with light,
      A kaleidoscope of color in abstract hue.
The glass collage conveys color so bright
      Saints are lined up in collinear review.

Each window a gateway to stories of sanctity,
      Every story refracted in a myriad of color.
Each ray of color replete with intensity
      Colors burst forth like a minute meteor.

Light of God from the sunlit world,
      A catalyst gives life to each window.
Tapestries of multi-hues strongly unfurl
      The church is enveloped in a spiritual glow.

Stained glass windows demonstrating scripture,
      The colors analogous to the artist's paint palette.
Depicting how holy men and women endured
      How they lived their faith and became saints.

When I Pray in Church

When I pray in Church
The silence sings very beautifully
When I pray in Church
The stained glass windows all smile at me wondrously
When I pray in Church
The light laden with color beams in on the cross bearing Jesus
When I pray in Church
The saints stop and look at me as if they were saying
"Welcome to my spiritual home"

The Narrow Door to Heaven

It is difficult to pass through the narrow door,
The one that opens to eternal life
Pride and self-centeredness add girth.
It is the fat that adds to the challenge.

Pomposity and egotism increase the width.
The load of self-importance impedes progress.
Ambition and intolerance add to the size.
Only humility will assist in size reduction.

Many rely on the shoehorn of false piety.
The panacea of insincere charity prevails.
Love of neighbor extended for prestige,
All are obstacles for entrance through the door.

God wants us to be with Him in heaven.
He wants us to experience the great joy.
He wants us to shed the cloak of materialism,
And reduce with a diet of love and good works.

Only then will the narrow door be accessible
To those who prioritize their spiritual goals.
To come closer to God, we shed all that impedes,
As we change, the door changes and we can enter.

(Inspiration for the poem came from a homily delivered during daily Mass. The door was built by the early Benedictine monks during construction of the historic Saint Meinrad Archabbey Church.)

Gateway to a Renewed Life

The New Year is but a gateway
    That we all must pass through.
To seize the opportunity to change
    Where our promise to God is renewed.

Why not a different New Year?
To promise to share Christ's love each day,
To our neighbors we give ourselves away.
We emulate Christ and for this we pray.

As we pass through the gateway once more
    We realize that we are not at the center.
God gives us charity and hope for tomorrow,
    With His Grace we invite Christ to enter.

The New Year is but a gateway to more blessings
    God's presence is ever beside us as before.
To once again have the opportunity for change,
    Our promise for renewal we cannot ignore.

Our neighbors often await us on the other side
    All we have to do is to open the gate.
We pass through with compassion, charity and love,
    Opportunities for ministry in the New Year await.

(Inspiration for the poem has come after experiencing countless decades of
encountering the New Year and making resolutions.)

GROWING CLOSER TO GOD

Angels at the Altar

I am the Clay You are the Potter

God's Eternal Love

Good Father, God

Reaching for the Stars

To be Unheralded Saints

I Greet the Morning

Blessings and Praise

His Presence Made Known

Advent of Winter

Angels at the Altar

The human eye cannot see them
      but the human heart can feel them.
They surround the celebrant like a cloak
      their grace and love blanket the altar.
Angels at the altar

Angels are in the pews with the faithful
      each and everyone has an angel beside him.
They guard and guide each worshipper
      to each the assignment originates with God.
Angels at the altar

Angels accompany the ministers in procession
      they guide the procession to the Eucharistic table.
Angels are encountered throughout the Church
      the Church is where they do their best work.
Angels at the altar

They are present throughout the Liturgy
      they recess the Church with the congregation.
They move to the streets and sidewalks
      their work in the secular world is unceasing.
Angels at the altar

I am the Clay You are the Potter

I am the clay and you are the potter
Take me and shape me and make me, O God
For I am the clay and you are the potter
From the womb before I was born you knew me
My life was pre-destined by you as the creator.

I am the clay and you are the potter
Give me the strength to accept what you send
Shaped in your image although I was weak
I was lost in my pride and my self-centered ego
Molded on the outside but hollow on the inside.

I am the clay and you are the potter
Shape me and mold me and teach me humility
Scrape away all the arrogant ways that I have
Help me search deep inside for weakness and greed
You can do all things for you are the master potter.

I am the clay and you are the potter
Give me eyes with the vision to see what I can be
To live up to be the best possible version of myself
The version that you have preordained me to be
That I can humbly start on the journey to you.

(Inspiration for this poem followed a homily by a pastor.)

God's Eternal Love

God's eternal love
    that no one can explain.
It is composed of deep devotion
    enriched by our sacrifice and pain.

God's eternal love is decisively unconditional
    it is endless and completely unselfish.
It endures unrelenting trials every day
    we offer up our cup for Him to replenish.

God's eternal love is patient and forgiving
    for all whose hope is forsaken.
It never dies or falters
    for believers whose faith awakens.

God's eternal love glows like the rarest gem
    it is a lamplight for our destination.
Never dimmed by some who lose their way
    God's eternal love defies all explanation.

God's eternal love is a many splendor miracle
    that many of us may not fully understand.
It is a wonderful truth and proof
    of His ever present healing hand.

Good Father, God

Good Father, God
    My life is in your hands
Open the door to heaven
    To provide what I need today
Even before my prayer is on my lips
    You know what it will be
    For shoes
    A decent job
Protection
    Help for those I love
    Hope for the future
Take care of me again today
And keep me very close to you
So that one day
    I may see you open Heaven's door
    To welcome me home.

Reaching for the Stars

In the world of chaos and strife
   it is difficult to try
To keep our moral values
   and our spirituality high...

We are chastised and ridiculed
   by the self-acclaimed sophisticate
Who proclaims with calloused tongue
   that such posture is really out of date...

But life is not worth living
   unless it is founded on God's truth
     And we build our moral foundation
      on the trials and errors of our youth...

     Let no one deny or hinder you there
     from designing a foundation of morality
     Composed of love, faith, humility and prayer
     always reminded that heightened
     spirituality...

     Is like reaching for the stars on high
     we may never reach them in life
Shining luminously high in the sky
   still we persist and prevail in our strife...

Realizing that God knows that we try
   that continuous conversion is the course
That will aid us in our journey to God on high
   and our spirituality will be the guiding force...

To be Unheralded Saints

We are destined by God to be saints
God challenges us to a holy openness
Finding God in the painful and the pleasant
God calls us all to a holy receptiveness.
To be unheralded saints

God calls us to be imperfect saints on each corner
To perceive His constant living presence there
A presence felt in every corner of the world
A constant commitment to being who you are.
To be unheralded saints

God call us to be saints with open arms
Embracing everything about being human
A calling that risks loving all people
A love knowing no bounds, safe limits or fear.
To be unheralded saints

God gives us the gift of imperfection
To enter into holy combat with forces of evil
Imperfection that is necessary to God's plans
Making imperfect unheralded saints on each corner.
To be unheralded saints

(Inspiration for this poem came on a street corner in Cairo, Egypt.)

I Greet the Morning

I greet the morning
From the mighty strength of the Trinity
Through a belief in the three-ness
Through an acceptance of oneness
Of God the creator of creation.

I greet the morning
Through God's strength to guide me
God's might to support me
God's wisdom to direct me
God's eye to see beyond me
God's word to direct my speech
From the snares of my enemies
From all those who hate me
Near and distant
Singular and in numbers.

I greet the morning
Through the strength of the Nativity
Through the power of His baptism
Through the strength of His resurrection
Through the strength of His ascension.

I greet the morning

Blessings and Praise

Lord

I praise you

for the blessing of natural beauty in my life

    pinnacled mountains from which your help comes

    green meadow valleys where I can walk without fear

    sun drenched fields that stretch the horizon

        with your abundant grace

Lord

I praise you

for the blessing of people in my life

    friends who know us

    and

    still love us

opponents who force us

    to examine our beliefs

    and

    accept theirs

Lord

I praise you

for the blessing of spirituality in my life

    prayers that give peaceful calm

    your grace just keeps coming

        unconditional love that will not be stilled

His Presence Made Known

I cannot see Him
Nor can I touch Him
Yet He is always there
Supporting always.

I can see were He hides
On the soft breeze
In the ripple of water
Rustling of leaves.

Presence made known
In a myriad of ways
On strips of rain
With snowfall in winter.

His grace abounds
In all of His creation
With waves of grain
By the horn of bounty.

He is the light in darkness
The pathway ever defined
My steps are sure and firm
To live in the truth forever.

Advent of Winter

Where do I look for God ?
>Do I look upward to the sky above?
Is He there in the ever-changing clouds?
>Is it there that I find His love?

Do I look for God in the wind that blows?
>Is He in the rustling of the fall foliage?
Do I seek His hand that colors autumn leaves?
>Is He always present on nature's stage?

Can God be in the animals that face winter?
>Does his hand guide their preparations?
Does God open nature's horn of plenty?
>Are all creatures allowed their due portions?

Is God with farmers who harvest their crops?
>Can I find Him in the cornfields and the grain?
Is God in the hay bales as they are stored in barns?
>Do I find God in all who ready for winter's quarantine?

Can God be found on majestic mountaintops?
>Is his image reflected in the still lake water?
Is He among the flowers that bloom with quiet beauty?
>Do I look for Him in nature's expansive theater?

A quiet voice is heard inside the ear of my mind.
>"Look for me ever closer inside your heart,
You will find me always there first and foremost.
>Then look for the works of my hand."

(Inspiration came from the advent of winter and God's presence in it.)

FAITH THROUGH THE SEASONS

Daystar of Eternal Joy

The angel Gabriel appeared before the young woman Mary
    With extraordinary news that was simple and profound
Unsettling news that was to change the Virgin Mary's life
    How could a woman of pure chastity have a virgin birth?
Daystar of Eternal Joy

Joseph did not understand the message but insisted on a journey
    On a donkey ride to Bethlehem escaping persecution
A puzzled innkeeper offered a stable as a temporary hospice
    Amidst the sweet smelling hay and warm animals.
Daystar of Eternal Joy

During labor preparation a bright light shone above
    Behold there was born a daystar of eternal joy
A bright star of deepest night guided the curious
    Radiating light of hope and salvation for humankind.
Daystar of Eternal Joy

Shepherds of the field came to offer homage
      To the daystar of eternal joy shining for humanity
Magi coming from the East bearing gifts for the daystar
      Guided by a shining star that illumined deepest night.

Daystar of Eternal Joy

Behold the brightness of the daystar of eternal joy
      Look and see it shining forth shafts of radiant light
His birth day when God in infinite wisdom grants true peace
      Giving hope and confidence to all who dwell upon earth.

Daystar of Eternal Joy

God's Gift of Winter

My God
We thank you for your gift
the gift of the cleansing power of winter
    the snow covered fields that quietly rest
    frozen ponds sheltering your aquatic creation
    snow laden hills that speak of your gentle embrace
        with your generous compassion.

My God
We praise you
for the protecting power of your love
    forgiveness for our transgressions
    the enhancement of our faith
    and
    renewal of our belief in salvation
    for the winter storms that precede the calm
    the healing power of cold
    of ice and frozen rain that lingers until spring
        its melting replenishing the earth.

My God
We sing of your glory
the power and might of wind and chill
    low grey clouds heavy with the frozen nectar of life
    nectar that harmonizes between sky and earth
    frost and cold that slows the hectic pace of humankind
    time for meditation and contemplative prayer
    and
    building anticipation for rebirth through warmth of the sun
        a resurrection not unlike that of your son.

My God
We praise your power
sleet and hailstones that rattle our windows
    the power of the wind moaning in the eaves
    weight of ice encrusted branches breaking
    breaking of limbs resounding like rifle shots
    in the stillness of the cold and still winter night
    scattering hoarfrost like ashes
    the white sheet of snow and frost enrobes your creation
        winter is a special time for rendering thanks to our Creator.

Signs of Christmas Night

Windowpanes reflecting joyful light
Fireplaces burning warm and bright,
Christmas trees standing straight and tall
These are some signs of Christmas Night.

Singers gathering to sing their carols
Voices praising Christ the child,
The sounds of Christmas tones sweet and low
Some are in Church to pray for a while.

Church bells ringing in the distance
Announcing the coming of the Savior,
Born in simple and humble surroundings
The birth is prophecy of love for neighbor.

Much joy and happiness abound
All the earth resounds as angels sing,
The Wise Men on camels follow the star
Treasures of frankincense and myrrh they bring.

The Christmas Star a great light in the heavens
Radiant and luminous rays light for the way,
Telling us to remember the most meaningful sign
The greatest story ever told compels us to pray.

Born in a little town called Bethlehem
The Christmas Star shines ever so bright,
An infant born to bring salvation into the world
All praise the Prince of Peace on Christmas night.

A Different Christmas

It is the Advent season and great joy erupts
Welling up to become praise and glory,
Manifested in the voices of believers
Carols and hymns toll out the great story.

A child is born of humble mortal lineage
A birth that fulfills the ancient prophecies,
The coming of a savior for all humankind
Prophecies predicted over many centuries.

Have we really felt the greatness of Christmas?
Christmas that is a true gift from God alone,
The gift of His only beloved son to all of us
The seed from the root of Jessie's stem is sown.

Be done with the ordinary Christmas season
A different Christmas where we give ourselves
away,
And have a joyous Christ-like Christmas
And pray that we share Christ's love each day.

(This poem was inspired by a shopping mall visit during a Christmas season
replete with noise, crowds, and very active consumerism.)

God's Winter Treasury

High above is a close grey winter sky
The brown leaves of the beeches still hang.
Most trees are barren of life-giving leaves
Branches covered with ice where birds once sang.

The snowflakes float gently downward
They are God's blessings for us all.
Formed from water droplets high above
God gave them symmetry and form as they fall.

No snowflakes are just like one another
God wanted them to be that way.
He welded them together as in a blanket
His gift of a white cathedral is for all to pray.

Under the blanket all life slumbers deep
The long winter night descends in cold splendor.
The cold winter moon forms patterns on the snow
The winter wind blows sharp as a razor.

God's power sends the great winds blowing
Sending misty veils of snow swirling upward.
God's might reflected in tree limbs snapping
Lashing of ice pellets are like a sharp-edged shard.

God's gift of winter is an infinite treasure of beauty
A gift from Him that is both majesty and apostleship.
The storm tones die away revealing tranquil silence
His gift is beauty incarnate and a thing to worship.

(Inspiration for this poem came from enduring the cold might of winter.)

An Image of Lent

The image of life as a journey
    Early people reflected on the meaning,
Of the earthly human existence
    Pilgrim journey spiritually beckons.
        An image of Lent

The image of the Christian's Lent
    Journey from Ash Wednesday to Easter,
Forty days analogous to the forty days
    Jesus spent fasting and praying.
        An image of Lent

The inward journey of conversion
    Most important of all of our journeys,
Always serving this inward journey
    Are almsgiving, self-denial, and prayer.
        An image of Lent

Lent, an inward journey with Christ
    Into the innermost truth of ourselves,
Facing the brokenness and imperfections
    Finding at our center the Living God.
        An image of Lent

God Gives Us Winter with the Blessing of Spring

Spring is the time when joy and hope draw ever near
  there is beauty all about us to see, touch and hear.
God sees that we may be downhearted and depressed
  He sends us trees with budding leaves to be addressed.

God gives the miracle of flowers pushing up through the ground
  the flower opens wide with unfurling petals making no sound.
It is just God's way of saying, "believe unfailingly in me"
  embrace the springtime budding of your favorite tree.

The darkness of your spirit will melt like the winter snow
  listen with the ear of your heart to the warm wind blow.
All winter's darkness will disappear as the bluebells ring
  God never gives us winter without the blessing of spring.

(Inspiration for the poem came from looking out a window during a grey
and bleak winter day.)

Some Thoughts on Lent

Lent is a penitential season:
> The Church prepares itself spiritually for Lent
> All brightly colored banners are taken down
> All vestiges of flowers and plants are removed
> A solemn sobriety descends like a pall.

Lent is a time for repentance:
> Ash Wednesday heralded the start of Lent
> We are to pray in the quiet of our inner rooms
> Praying from the heart and not the mouth
> This we do in terms of fasting and almsgiving.

Lent is a time for sacrifice:
> We are not to seek praise from others
> Avoid being like the hypocrites who fasted openly
> Changing their appearance for the look of fasting
> With humility we pray to our God without fanfare.

Lent is a journey:
> For we are truly dust and to dust we will return
> The material wealth and fame will be left behind
> We are all pilgrims striving to grow closer to God
> Lent is but a pilgrimage on the way to the kingdom.

Lent is a time for prayer:
> Embrace each day of Lent with fervent prayer
> That the resurrected Lord will become our guide
> Mortal life is fleeting so give thanks for the gift of life
> God's only son died for us so that we can live eternally.

(The beginning of Lent gave impetus to this poem.)

God's Presence

The sky and the stars, the sea and the waves
The dew on the grass and the leaves on the trees
A gurgling brook carrying snow melt water
The birds on the wing migrate northward.
Announce the presence of God

The movement of a leaf initiated by a soft wind
The mantle of exploding flowers covering meadows
A cacophony of nature's myriad sounds reverberate
Insects and amphibians play their musical instruments.
Announce the presence of God

Land becomes alive and the earth begins to breathe
Green as a color begins to intensify the landscape
Waterways and marshes resound with sounds of life
The migration northward pulsates with vast numbers.
Announce the presence of God

The miracle of life so evident in nature's diverse species
Perpetuation of the species is so clearly observed
Once barren the landscape is full of reproductive activity
God the architect of the earth fills it with many wonders.
Announce the presence of God

Lent is:

Lent is:
a penitential season
formation of the Paschal Mystery
        for
                baptism
                confirmation
                first Eucharist
                spiritual formation
                commitment to beliefs

Lent is:
a time for giving up some of the good things in life
        for
                prayer
                fasting
                almsgiving

Lent is:
a time for sacrifice
        for
                a beautiful gift to God
                life giving water in the desert of Lent
                death of a way of life
                experiencing who we are

Lent is:
a time for repentance
        for
                taking up our daily cross
                receiving the Holy Spirit
                turning away from complacency
                turning to God with our whole heart.

(The Lenten season provided inspiration for this poem.)

The Signs of God's Hands in Spring

Beneath an azure blue and washed cloudless sky
      is seen a canopy and carpet of verdant green
      vibrant in a crisp spring morning for all to see

   the signs of God's hands are seen everywhere
      birds resound their mating calls
      tree leaves are small and immature
      allowing sunlight to apply its life force
      small plants push upward through winter matted soil

   the signs of God's hands are seen everywhere
      only yesterday the ground was barren and frozen
      small animals emerge from winter habitats
      waterways begin to murmur and gurgle
      snow melt and winter rains provide a force

   the signs of God's hands are seen everywhere
      marshes come alive with escalating activity
      beneath the water life forms are energized
      the fields are smiling and woods are alive with blossoms
      an aura of quiet peaceful roaring in the wood

   the signs of God's hands are seen everywhere
      in the spring rains that promise baptism and renewal
      in the peacefulness of spring woods as cloistered solitude
      with the insects beginning their chorus of song sound
      bursting buds and flower heads turned to the face of God

Beneath an azure blue and washed cloudless sky
      a green sea of tranquility and perfect peace
      beckons to all who heed and listen attentively

God's Awakening Call

All of nature hears God's call of spring

    His resounding call wakes up everything

During winter all appears dead and still

    now rises to life amid the bird's trill

God turns everything green with a magical hand

a beautiful mantle spreads across the fertile land

How can anyone resist this vibrant awakening call

and not watch the swelling buds on trees so tall

Or witness a fern erupting upward and through

    and flower stalks pushing upward too

Just yesterday the ground was barren and frozen

    God's awakening call heeded by all that are chosen

All that are sleeping beneath the ground

    come to life as they hear the awakening sound

They push upward to meet the warmth of the risen sun

    we too reach upward toward the warmth of God's son

Nature's own resurrection analogous to Christ's own

    salvation provided through the verdant crown

Listen with the ear of the heart to God's awakening call

    we, like flowering plants awaken in perpetual renewal

Because some day we will be called from earthly sleep

    to ascend the ladder to a place so high and steep

We heed God's call to a place where there is eternal life

    where saints and angels sing and we are free from strife.

God Gave Us

God gave us the foliage of trees
    He gave us the earth
    To nurture and care for it
God gave us spring flowers
    Wild bluebells and dandelions
    That rise up to greet the morning sun
God gave us the sweet air of spring
    The trill of bird songs
    Crescendo of insect sounds
God gave us the sweet balm of spring
    Tremulous leaves on majestic trees
    Warm breezes that caress the cheeks

God gave us the gift of hearing
    To hear the frogs sounding in the marsh
    The shrill call of red winged blackbirds
    Their rising and falling lends rhythm
    To all forms of life
God gave us the gift of life
    Accepting stewardship in His name
    Evangelizing through an active lifestyle
    To perpetuate love to all His creation.

God's Gift of Summer

All of nature acknowledges the advent of summer

    God has awakened everything and growth is eminent

The warmth of the sun and warm summer rains

    Summer has placed a magic hand on God's creation.

How can one not lie back and gaze on the azure summer sky

    Trace the billowy clouds as they constantly change

The earth begins to dry out from incessant spring rains

    Life is a mixture of sunshine and rain as a gift of God's love.

The sky and stars, dew on the grass and the leaves on trees

    The constant reminders of God's presence and love

Summer is a time when God proclaims the work of His hands

    God is as close as the wind that caresses a face.

Summer is a season of quiet development and growth

    Flowers bloom in their fragrance from the hand of the giver

Summer is just another room in the temple of God

    Each seasonal room is a place for silent prayer.

God's Gift of Autumn

God's autumn is a gift with a purpose
Without death there can be no resurrection
No possible journey into the eternal life

So it is with God's design of nature
Most vegetation begins a journey
A journey guided into a dormant state.

Leaves fall and their life giving energy
Takes a hiatus from food production
To resume again with increased sunlight

Animals begin their hibernation for winter
Some gather food for winter sustenance
All life prepares for inanimate suspension.

God in His creative design has provided
For a period of slowing the tempo of life
To renew the life cycle with renewed energy

Autumn of the human life is analogous
To God's gift of benevolence through autumn
Death is a prelude to the resurrection of eternal life.

PROCLAMATION OF FAITH

The Sign of the Cross

Courage Born of Faith

Faith Comes Gift-Wrapped

Go in Peace

Faith Holds it to My Lips

Faith is the Color of Red

I Lit a Candle Today

To Have Faith

God's Own Signature

The Sign of the Cross

It is a symbolic manual gesture
    A simple ritual hand motion
Tracing of the Cross on Calvary
    Marking the four points of the Cross.

It replicates Jesus Christ's crossing
    From His own death unto life
Moving from Hades to Paradise
    Always symbolizing the Trinity.

Spoken or a mental recitation
    Following a Trinitarian formula
Belief in God as three identities
    The Father, Son and Holy Spirit.

The symbolism of Christ's cross
    Two lines intersecting at right angles
A cross easily discernible to the viewer
    It is overt sign to all of a strong faith.

Be not ashamed to trace His cross
    One who willingly gave His life for us
Letting the world know of our deep love
    His death on the Cross is our salvation.

(Inspiration for this poem has always existed in liturgical and devotional prayer.)

Courage Born of Faith

No one should have to bury their children,
    it is not supposed to be that way.
Those words from a grieving father,
    words tempered by a deep faith.

Heeding the request of a dying child,
    asking the father to officiate at the funeral.
As an ordained deacon to celebrate a life,
    how difficult it must have been.

Words of the homily were heart-rending,
    there were no words more knowing.
A message so consoling with God's presence,
    giving a time map from creation to redemption.

Homiletic offering delivered with a contrite heart,
    its great strength was love and defiance of despair.
Guided by God whose greatest passion is compassion,
    courage born of faith turned familial grief to Him.

(Inspiration for this poem came during a funeral service for the daughter of a
fellow parishioner and friend.)

Faith Comes Gift-Wrapped

Faith comes to us gift-wrapped
    It is wrapped with the cross of Christ
It is a special gift from God
    We accept His gift and do not resist.

It is easy to say in God we trust
    When everything is going our way
But when confronted by trials and hardships
The gift of faith unwrapped is our mainstay.

The gift of faith is wrapped
    In the folds of Jesus' passion
His sacrifices and endurance of pain
    The darkness dispelled by His benefaction.

The gift of faith enables us to endure what comes
    Strengthened by our self discipline in prayer
Nurtured by the gift bestowed upon us
    The gift of faith is our shield of power.

There are many gifts that are wrapped
    But none is greater than the gift of faith
Unwrapped it becomes a block of strength
    It is a gift born of God's love for our rebirth.

(Inspiration for this poem came from a homily given by a seminarian of Saint Meinrad School of Theology and a summer intern at St. Charles.)

Go in Peace

Sacrament of reconciliation
    a hidden power
        promotes healing and restoration
            removes barriers of sin
                Go in Peace

A great gift from God
    opens us up to the interior being
        reaching the depths of our inner soul
            the mind is transformed and renewed
            Go in Peace

Confession is
    not just for the big transgressions
        reception to Grace of sinning no more
            grace to deal with false inner drives
            Go in Peace

Sacrament with vision
    increased hope of greater union with Jesus
        opens us up to greater interior healing
            hope for a change in our lives
            Go in Peace

Confession through the Cross
    humility before the Cross can heal
        liberation reaches to the depth of the self
            power of the Cross brings new freedom
            Go in Peace

(This poem emanated from the question "Why Reconciliation?" that was proposed by a recent convert.)

Faith Holds it to My Lips

The cup I raise up with my hands
    I press my lips to the rim
Taking a small sip I say Amen
    The blood of Christ is my strength.

I do not know how the wine is transformed
    It is a mystery beyond my understanding
I do know that it is food for my soul
    This is enough until I meet Jesus.

At that time all mysteries will be revealed
    It is enough that Jesus is a part of me
The consecration becomes the pillar of strength
    Faith holds the cup to my lips.

(Inspiration came from observing others avoiding the cup consistently.)

Faith is the Color of Red

Faith is the color of red

God

Is unwilling to be ignored

And man

Cannot remain forever impervious

To what God longs to bestow

Those who cannot keep secular quests balanced

Find themselves at times

Beyond the sight of the unseen

And fail to be illumined by God's love

There are those who color red

Others wear a mask

In the presence of God.

(Inspiration came from wonderment at the amount of the color red used by the Roman Catholic Church during Mass and other sacramental services.)

I Lit a Candle Today

I lit a candle in church today
No one was there to see it
The match flickered its tongue
The soft wick ignited into a yellow flame.

        I lit a candle today

I recited a prayer of intention
It rose upward with the candle smoke
It rose upward like incense conveying my prayer
It was a prayer of peace and of healing.

        I lit a candle today

I know that God sees the light from the flame
A light that beams hope from the gleaming taper
My prayer rises to God borne on candle smoke
And God answers in His time and not mine.

        I lit a candle today

(This poem is in response to the conflict between the Palestinians and the Israelis in Gaza and for an end to the hostilities.)

To Have Faith

To have faith is to believe that there is a living God
    Faith to believe that He cares deeply for our pain
To have faith is to deny logic and completely trust in God
    Faith to believe that He will be present and help us
To have faith

To have faith is to act courageously and face our fears
    Faith to believe in life, in ourselves, and in the world
To have faith is to believe that we can prosper and succeed
    Faith to believe in ourselves after enduring failures
To have faith

To have faith is to believe in God and His promises
    Faith that through Jesus He fulfilled His love for us
To have faith is to believe we can keep our hopes alive
    Faith that we can build confidence and overcome doubts
To have faith

To have faith is to believe the truth of God's word
    Faith that is based on truth that brings us closer to God
To have faith that without it we can never find peace with God
    Faith that will assist us to live the complete life with joy
To have faith

God's Own Signature

God signed His name in the sky last night,
Reflected in the stars above, His autograph was bright.
He signed His name in the fields with the morning dew,
His signature was in the rising sun bringing light anew.

The golden sign of His presence was awesome to behold,
He wrote His name in the sunlight, an autograph of gold.
The fragrance of God was manifested in flowers along my way,
God's sign was on the breeze that gently caressed me today.

He signed His name with the kiss of the sun on my cheek,
Speaking to me of His eternal love, urging me not to be weak.
It was a day of happiness and a moment that He reassures,
His signature on all the world is a sign that His love endures.

The fading twilight sweeps across the evening sky,
God's sign is visible in the trees and the clouds so high.
God's signature illuminates warmth of compassion and light,
For He made the world and all things in it to shine bright.

CLOTHED FOR THE JOURNEY

A Time for Me to Leave

Bread for the Journey

God Has Thrown Us a Lifeline

Prayers Are the Steps Leading to God

Greet Every Day with Joy

Surrender to God

The Convert

The Cross in My Pocket

The Garment of Salvation

The Sound of Silence is Heard

A Time for Me to Leave

It is now the time for me to leave
    But it will be for only a little while.
I heed the call of my Father do not grieve
    Embrace my passing on with a smile.

We have shared much in this mortal life,
    The hardships, sufferings and pain endured.
Our faith in God has diminished the strife
    Remember the spiritual journey God nurtured.

It is time to believe in God's mercy and grace
    He leads through the gateway to eternal life.
This is the last leg of an earthly race
    The race has ended and diminished the strife.

It is time for the living to move on,
    Remember not to grieve nor shed sad tears.
See another side to pain and move beyond
    Sublimate your sorrow and travel the years.

(This poem was written as the writer reflected on his
mortality as well as that of his family and friends.)

Bread for the Journey

Bread has been the staple of life for countless centuries
The baking of bread a sacred daily familial routine
Pilgrims on a journey carried bread as the staff of life
Bread saturated with a nourishing broth gave strength.
Bread for the Journey

The Church is the mixing bowl where the bread is shaped
The yeast of our faith connects us with God's creation
Punching down the dough before the kneading and rising
So too do we get punched down before rising again.
Bread for the Journey

So it is with us who live in contemporary times
Ingredients are mixed with good yeast for the dough
The yeast of faith helps us to rise like the bread
Love of God and for neighbor are basic ingredients.
Bread for the Journey

The Israelites received manna sent down by God
Our manna is faith and compassionate service to others
Like the bread for the journey faith sustains us
The temperature of good works is the baking force.
Bread for the Journey

(Inspiration for this poem was a retreat presented by Fr. Gabriel, OSB, at Saint Meinrad Archabbey.)

God Has Thrown Us a Lifeline

God has thrown to each of us a spiritual lifeline
In the darkest of night when life's storm is at its worst
God has offered us a lifeline in our drowning moments
The lifeline connects us with God and to each other.

The trials and strife of our daily secular life
Bring us down into the abysses of deep darkness
God's gift of prayer is a connection to Him
Prayer that is the lifeline of salvation He has thrown.

In moments of desperation and deep sorrow
The lifeline of prayer such as the Holy Rosary
Beseeches the Virgin Mary to intercede for us
God often assigns the throwing of a lifeline to others.

When anxiety matches the intensity of life's storms
When high winds rattle the windows of our souls
Just when the tempest of life threatens us the most
The lifeline to God is thrown for each of us to catch.

(Inspiration came from meditative reflection during a retreat held at Saint Meinrad Archabbey.)

Prayers Are the Steps Leading to God

Prayers are the steps leading to God
They make up the glorious staircase
We must climb the steps every day
It is the upward ascent we must face.

Prayers are the steps that lead to the Lord
To meet the Lord in prayer is our reward
We pass through the door of the house of prayer
If we persevere we find God waiting there.

The house of prayer is never far away
At the foot of the staircase we kneel to pray
God is in our hearts and He is with us all the way
God's angels climb with us to the eternal doorway.

Prayers are the steps that bring us closer to God
Our spiritual fitness enables us to climb to Him
Our faith carries us upward as we fervently plod
Heaven looms majestically as we cross over the brim.

(Inspiration for the poem came from a homily given by a Deacon in Lake Zurich, IL.)

Greet Every Day with Joy

Greet every day with great joy
Be ever grateful for the gift of life
Our life is temporal and short-lived
Know God with simple and joyful delight.

We are surrounded with God's creation
Ask Him to guide us as we look
To find beauty in others and in ourselves
Listen for the sounds of birds or soft wind.

Look for flower blooms in nature's treasure trove
All nurtured in the warmth of a sun-filled day
Feel the undulating wind on your face
Conveying the laughter of children at play.

We are all pilgrims on the journey of life
The pilgrimage is fleeting and quickly ends
Knowledge of this pierces like a knife
All that remains are our good and bad deeds.

Then we are truly dust and to dust we return
All accumulated power, riches and fame diminish
We are one with the poorest of the poor
Now God's gate to heaven opens and we can enter.

(Inspiration for this poem came about because of age, an increased knowledge
about our mortality, and the need to find joy in God.)

Surrender to God

In our ordinary day-to-day life
    Our surrender to God becomes spiritual.
We are given a choice despite earthly strife
    Making the yes or no choice to God habitual.

The word surrender implies a negative feeling
    It can be raising a white flag or being a loser.
The act of surrendering is contradictory to winning
    It is unpopular because it implies a quitter.

God gives His love to all who passionately love Him
    Yet many resist God's love because of fears.
An integral part of surrender is trust in God as a maxim
    Giving up control and self-will should bring no tears.

Emptying ourselves we can make room for Him
    It is then that God can be the supreme ramrod.
Spiritual surrender brings us up to His eternal brim
    It is just a simple matter of saying yes or no to God.

(Inspiration for the poem came from a theme in a retreat given by Fr. Vincent Tobin, OSB, monk of Saint Meinrad Archabbey.)

The Convert

She was born into a different faith
    complying with the dictates of inheritance.
Accepting the birthright of Christianity
    moving through a standard of familial acceptance.

Swinging in and out of devotional services
    meeting some with dark desolation.
Struggling to find a balance of rhythm and truth
    often finding just solitary spiritual isolation.

Occasionally finding direction through God's spiritual hand
    soothing her restless soul and leading her onward.
She waited with impatience and listened with her heart
    for advice that was both honest and straightforward.

One day a visitation to a tradition rich Church
accepting the evangelization of a trusted companion.
Sensing the surge of righteousness and truth in the Eucharist
realizing the necessity of conversion and of opposition.

Emerging from the rigors of preparation
filled with the Holy Spirit fanning spiritual activism.
Impatient to become the best possible disciple of
    Christ
knowing that God's love is the epitome of altruism.

(This poem was inspired by the conversion of a young
friend.)

The Cross in My Pocket

There is a little cross in my pocket
    I placed it there for a purpose.
It is there to remind me of my Savior
    He is the one whose blood was shed for me.

I carry the cross and touch it with my fingers
    It helps me to pray and to remember Jesus.
It is a small little cross without a chain
    Oh yes, I have a cross around my neck.

This cross is often inaccessible to me
    The cross in my pocket is always accessible.
Sometimes I take it out of my pocket
    I hold it in my hand and remember His passion.

The cross in my hand is not visible to others
    This is not why I carry this little cross.
I carry the cross to remember the Son of God
    And the magnificent sacrifice He made for me.

(The small cross that the writer carries was given to him at a Cursillo Men's Weekend Retreat many years ago.)

The Garment of Salvation

We are called to put on
the garment of salvation
God wants us to wear
this clothing everyday
put on the robe of holiness
and righteousness of truth
clothe ourselves with virtues
that will support our transformation

Clothe ourselves with psalms,
hymns and prayers
from the moment of baptism
we are clothed
with the garment of the Holy Spirit
we are called to put on the clothing
of Christ each day
just as we physically dress ourselves
each and every morning

We are called to put on our new self
created in God's way
of righteousness and truth
the spiritual clothing will have
a great effect on those around us
it is the only garment we will need
for our journey to God
the garment will grow more resplendent
as we grow spiritually

The Sound of Silence is Heard

The sound of silence is heard
> In the recesses of the church
> In the cloister of the abbey
> In the desert of the mind

The sound of silence is heard
> On the wings of the blowing wind
> With the heart whispers of the soul
> In the monk's contemplative prayer

The sound of silence is heard
> In the meditative prayer of the pious
> In the music of the soaring soul
> In the inaudible sound of the contrite heart

The sound of silence is heard
> Silence heard with the ear of the heart
> In the quiet flickering of a prayer candle
> In candle flames dispelling the darkness

The sound of silence is heard
> In the wonderful sense of God's presence
> In the solidarity place of personal prayer
> In silence heard in the seeking of God

(A visit to Gethsemani Abbey, a Trappist Monastery in
Kentucky, inspired this poem.)

THE SON OF GOD

Joseph Answered God's Call

My Lord God

He Carried His Cross

Holy Savior, My Lord

I Took a Walk with Jesus Today

The Miracle of the Cup

On the Road to Calvary

Encountering Jesus

O Sun of God

The Imprint of Jesus

Hiding Places of Jesus

Joseph Answered God's Call

What was it like, Joseph
When an angel of God spoke to you.
Did you feel apprehension or doubt
When you felt unwarranted deception.
Joseph answered God's call

What was it like, Joseph
Supporting Mary in the birth of God's Son.
Acceptance of raising Him as a child
Holding Him always close to your heart.
Joseph answered God's call

What was it like, Joseph
When you escaped to Egypt with family
Securing sanctuary in a foreign land.
Returning to Israel with Mary and Jesus
So that He could fulfill His destiny.
Joseph answered God's Call

What was it like, Joseph
Accepting Jesus as your earthly Son.
To teach Him to work with wood
To support and stand by Him.
Joseph answered God's call

(Inspiration came from looking at St. Joseph's statue in churches. St. Joseph's decision to remain as husband/father epitomizes the faith and trust in God.)

My Lord God

My Lord God
Heal my wounded soul.

I know that of all creation
Only the family of humans
Has veered off the pathway leading to you
I know that we humans are the ones
Who are separated from one another
And we are the only ones
Who can decide to unite as one body
And walk on the pathway leading to you.

My Lord God
Most holy one
Instruct us in your love, compassion and grace
That we may use your gift of healing
        And heal our world
        And heal each other.

He Carried His Cross

He carried the cross to Calvary
   Pilgrims all we also carried the same
We went the way He did long ago
   Pilgrims fervently prayed in His name.

Faith in our hearts we walk the path He trod
   He carried His cross as a burden for us
Knowing through prayer it is the way to God
   Salvation and forgiveness of sins His focus.

The burden of the cross lay heavy on our backs
   Jesus' burden of the cross was even heavier
Sins of the whole world was a personal rack
   The weight of the wood pierced like a rapier.

Via Dolorosa is known as the way of pain
   To walk this way becomes our spiritual gain
Never did one feel Jesus' pain more than this day
   Blessed are we to carry a cross in His name.

(This poem is a reflection on a pilgrimage to the Holy Land and the Via Dolorosa.)

Holy Savior, My Lord

Holy Savior, my Lord,

      my life is in your hands.

Open the gate of heaven

      may you provide what I require today.

Even before my prayer is on my lips,

      You know what that prayer will be--

          for honest employment

          protection for my family

          help for those I love

          for a balanced prayer life

          security in the present

          hope for the future

      Reach out and take care of me today

          embrace me in your loving arms

          never let me stray from you

          let me see you in all that I meet

          may I hear you with the ear of my heart

          so that some day

I may see you at the portal to heaven

      waiting to welcome me to my eternal home.

I Took a Walk with Jesus Today

I took a walk with Jesus today
>We had a lot of things to talk about
We trekked through the Father's creation
>Our conversation pulsated with great joy.

His stride was strong and powerful
>It reflected His strength of character
I struggled to keep pace and be thankful
>I listened attentively to all of His words.

I focused with concentration on His words
>The gradual unfolding of this encounter
Revealed the love that the Father has for us
>That God's love can awaken joy within us.

Jesus strode on with an inner strength
>Energized by His all-encompassing love
His arm lightly encircled my shoulders
>Imparting to me His energized faith and love.

Jesus spoke of love of God and neighbor
>That our pilgrimage will lead us to the Father
That through Jesus we can grow closer to God
>If we heed the call to evangelization of others.

I told Jesus of my troubles and woes
>That there were times when life gave me much pain
He said His mortal life was often filled with pain
>I found solace knowing His pain was the greater.

The Miracle of the Cup

The cup is raised to my hands
The hands of the minister raised it up
I press my lips to the rim and sip
The blood of Christ becomes my strength.

I do not know just how it happens
As mysterious to me as the miracle at Cana
That the wine consecrated by the celebrant
Becomes food for my needy soul.

I am sure that someday I will know
That all mysteries will be explained
That if I have unconditional faith
The blood of Jesus will sustain me until then.

The cup is raised by my hands
And my faith is enough to believe
That the blood of Christ is my lifeline
Until I meet Him face to face with the Father.

(The Precious Blood as part of the Eucharist in the Mass inspired this poem.)

On the Road to Calvary

Jesus carried His cross to Calvary
His shoulders bore the burden for you and me
Nailed to the cross He was crucified
It was for us He endured the pain and died.

We too bear a cross whatever it may be
Accepting the burden will lead us to eternity
We can only pray and not despair
As we place our earthly strife in His care.

Evangelize with those who live the material life
Help them to conversion and release from strife
To become disciples of the risen Lord
Following His way to eternal life is a major reward.

Prayer and service to others is a stepping stone
To a life everlasting such as we have never known
Jesus carried His cross to show us the way
We'll follow His path to the everlasting eternal day

Encountering Jesus

A powerful force propelled me
To walk specifically down a tree-lined lane
An old farmhouse loomed up ahead.

I saw a figure sitting on the porch
A bearded man sat in a rocking chair
Another chair was unoccupied beside him.

He beckoned to me with his arm
He patted the seat beside him
An overt invitation to join him
A quiet acceptance came to me easily.

We sat in silence for a while
Looking out at God's creation
He spoke in a well-modulated voice
He said I was troubled and confused.

Trust in my Father's love completely
Turn yourself unconditionally over to Him
Allow me to guide you to His house
Follow my footsteps with a contrite heart.

I felt an arm on my shoulder
The touch of it assured me of love
I stood before Jesus just as I was
Ready for forgiveness and repentance.

O Sun of God

O Sun of God
You came to dispel the darkness
Your light makes the night bright
And heralds the joys of day.

O Sun of God
Your footprints lead us back
To life's true radiant grace
You are a lantern for our feet.

O Sun of God
You illuminate our journey
We are guided by your abundant love
Your light of love permeates our souls.

O Sun of God
The brilliant rays of your love for us
Penetrate to the depths of our hearts
Guiding us on our journey to your Father.

The Imprint of Jesus

The footsteps that He leaves
Are imprinted on the permeable soil
The ground must be soft to accept them
So too must our hearts be soft.

The footprints deepen as He moves
The weight of our problems assists
He carries them as He does us
The direction is always forward.

The pressure of a hand in mine
The strength emanates from Him
The hand supports and leads
It is a lasting imprint on my hand.

There is a gentle touch on my back
Supporting me as we move forward
Jesus leads and guides us with love
The journey to His father becomes easy.

The surface that we tread upon
Is made up of movable particles
At times they are grains of sand
We also become like grains of sand.

The imprint of His sacrifice overwhelms
Unconditional love for us is given
His words reiterated in the Scriptures
Imprint upon our accepting open minds.

Hiding Places of Jesus

Jesus hides most often in the least of places
A beggar on the street corner as traffic races
In the guise of the destitute and the poor
He challenges us to find Him in the obscure.

Hiding places can be diverse and concealing
Our faith enables us to see Him in the living
He lives within all creatures great and small
Butterflies on the wing and in the wild goose call.

Jesus lives in those who hate and abhor us
In the road rager who shouts and utters a curse
He lives in those who hate and those who love
Often selecting hiding places dictated from above.

We are to see Jesus in everyone we encounter
Rich and poor alike and those who flounder
Often it is difficult to discern the hiding places
He walks with a light tread and leaves no traces.

We are to open the door and admit all who knock
Not knowing where Jesus hides to test His flock
With our hearts open we will see Him clearly
He loves us unconditionally embracing us dearly.

The author's earlier poetry book, *Deepening Faith through Poetry*, is available for purchase on-line.

About the Artist

Br. Martin Erspamer, OSB, is a monk of Saint Meinrad Archabbey. He is a highly respected and well-known liturgical artist who has worked for many years in a variety of media and as an illustrator. He has worked in the media of stained glass windows where he has been highly successful. His other artistic skills include ceramics, painting, drawing, and furniture.

He has been always supportive of the oblate program at Saint Meinrad Archabbey and he has illustrated this book because of this interest. The book *The Work of Our Hands: The Art of Martin Erspamer* is a wonderful testimony to his creativity in liturgical art.

The illustrations presented in this book are deeply appreciated and sincere gratitude is extended to Br. Martin Erspamer, OSB, for his generous contribution of his artwork.

Made in the USA
Charleston, SC
06 March 2011